discovermore

Good Health

Proteins

Ursula Pang

Britannica Educational Publishing
IN ASSOCIATION WITH
THE ROSEN PUBLISHING GROUP

Published in 2027 by Britannica Educational Publishing (a trademark of Encyclopædia Britannica, Inc.) in association with The Rosen Publishing Group, Inc.
2544 Clinton Street, Buffalo, NY 14224

Distributed exclusively by Rosen Publishing.
To see additional Britannica Educational Publishing titles, go to rosenpublishing.com.

Editor: Greg Roza
Book Design: Michael Flynn

Photo Credits: Cover Ground Picture/Shutterstock.com; (series background) Dai Yim/Shutterstock.com; p. 5 (top) Farknot Architect/Shutterstock.com; p. 5 (bottom) PeopleImages/Shutterstock.com; p. 7 (top) Danijela Maksimovic/Shutterstock.com; p. 7 (bottom) Magic mine/Shutterstock.com; p. 8 ridersuperone/Shutterstock.com; p. 9 Elena Veselova/Shutterstock.com; p. 10 Birdiewithvalise/Shutterstock.com; p.11 Ekaterina Glazkova/Shutterstock.com; p. 13 (top) ustas7777777/Shutterstock.com; p. 13 (bottom) Photoroyalty/Shutterstock.com; p. 14 Dee-sign/Shutterstock.com; p. 15 StudioMolekuul/Shutterstock.com; p. 17 (top) MaraZe/Shutterstock.com; p. 17 (bottom) Kritchai7752/Shutterstock.com; p. 18 5PH/Shutterstock.com; p. 19 Oleksandr Yakoniuk/Shutterstock.com; p. 20 PhotoGranary02/Shutterstock.com; p. 21 Billy F Blume Jr/Shutterstock.com; p. 22 Farion_O/Shutterstock.com; p. 23 Toa55/Shutterstock.com; p. 24 Nelson Bastidas/Shutterstock.com; p. 25 Avatar_023/Shutterstock.com; p. 26 JLugonStudio/Shutterstock.com; p. 27 Jacek Chabraszewski/Shutterstock.com; p. 28 Cook Shoots Food/Shutterstock.com; p. 29 Vechterova Valeria/Shutterstock.com.

Cataloging-in-Publication Data

Names: Pang, Ursula.
Title: Proteins / Ursula Pang.
Description: Buffalo, New York : Britannica Educational Publishing, an imprint of Rosen Publishing, 2027. | Series: Discover more: good health | Includes glossary and index.
Identifiers: ISBN 9781641905954 (pbk.) | ISBN 9781641905961 (library bound) | ISBN 9781641905978 (ebook)
Subjects: LCSH: Proteins in human nutrition--Juvenile literature. | Food--Protein content--Juvenile literature.
Classification: LCC TX553.P7 P36 2027 | DDC 613.282--dc23

Manufactured in the United States of America

Some of the images in this book illustrate individuals who are models. The depictions do not imply actual situations or events.

CPSIA Compliance Information: Batch #CSBRIT27. For further information contact Rosen Publishing at 1-800-237-9932.

Contents

What Are Nutrients?

We eat food because we need nutrients. Nutrients are what a body requires to move, grow, and stay alive. All living things need nutrients to function. Plants make some nutrients and take in others from the air and soil. Animals, such as humans, get nutrients from the foods they eat.

Proteins, carbohydrates, fats, minerals, vitamins, and water are all nutrients. Proteins are needed for body tissue to grow and repair itself. After water and possibly fat, protein is the most abundant material in the human body.

Carbohydrates supply most of the energy the body needs. Fats store extra energy for the body. Minerals and vitamins keep the body healthy. Water has many uses in the body. In fact, water makes up most of the weight of the human body.

A balanced diet is one that contains more than just one kind of nutrient. Different foods contain different kinds and amounts of nutrients.

compareandcontrast

How is protein like the other kinds of nutrients? How is it different?

Protein keeps your body strong. About one-sixth of the body's total weight is protein.

Breaking Down Proteins

The human body uses proteins for many reasons. They include growth, movement, reproduction, repair, and digestion.

Proteins are made up of groups of molecules called amino acids. A molecule is the smallest unit of a substance that has all the properties of that substance. For instance, a water molecule is the smallest unit that is still water. Molecules are made of even smaller bits called atoms. Amino acid molecules consist of atoms of carbon, hydrogen, oxygen, nitrogen, and sometimes sulfur.

More than 100 kinds of amino acids are found in nature. However, only twenty kinds are the building blocks of all proteins in living things. Amino acids combine in various patterns to make different proteins.

This is a model of the amino acid valine.

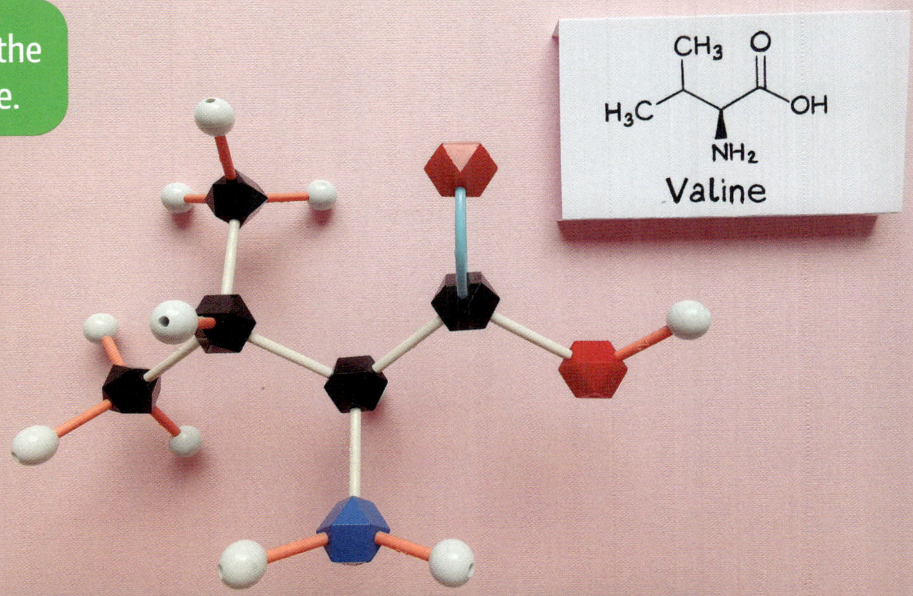

compare**and**contrast

How are molecules similar to atoms? How are they different?

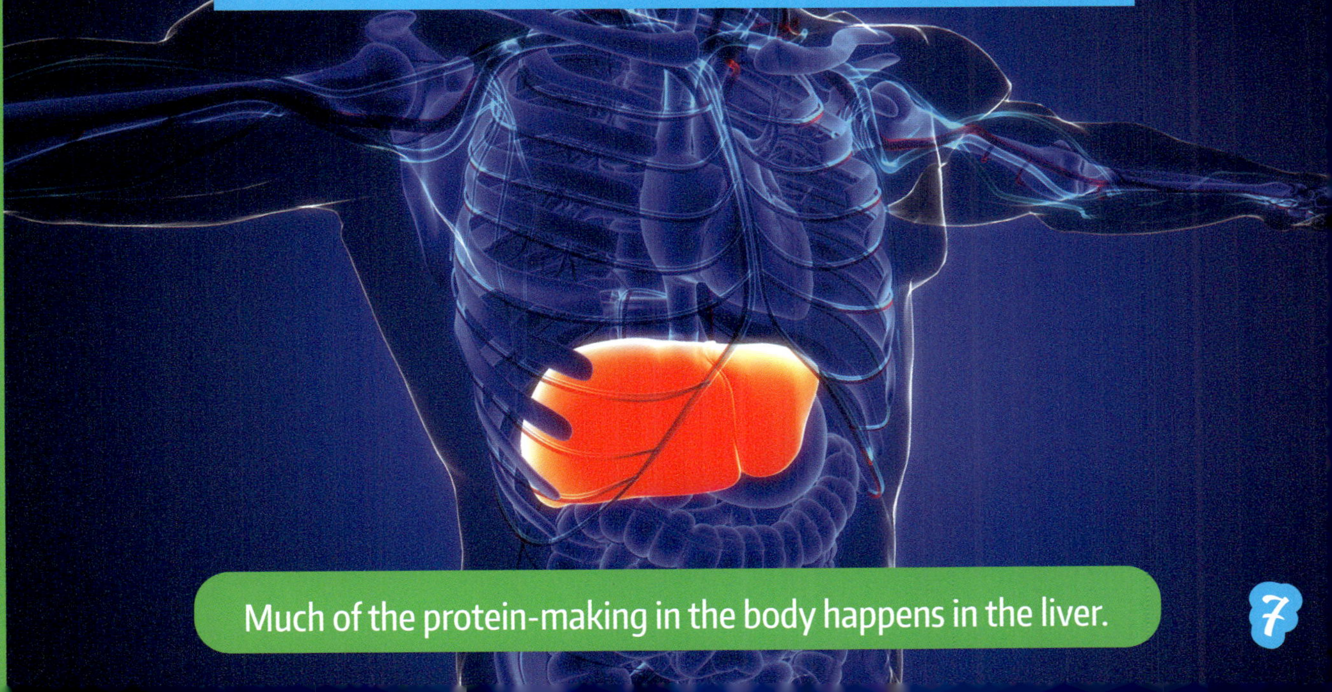

Much of the protein-making in the body happens in the liver.

While amino acids are made up of similar atoms, each protein has its own **sequence** of amino acids that determines the shape and function of the protein. This means that each protein has a specific mix of amino acids (including many repeating ones) arranged in a specific order.

Most common proteins contain more than 100 amino acids. For example, hemoglobin, a protein found in red blood cells, is made of 287 amino acids.

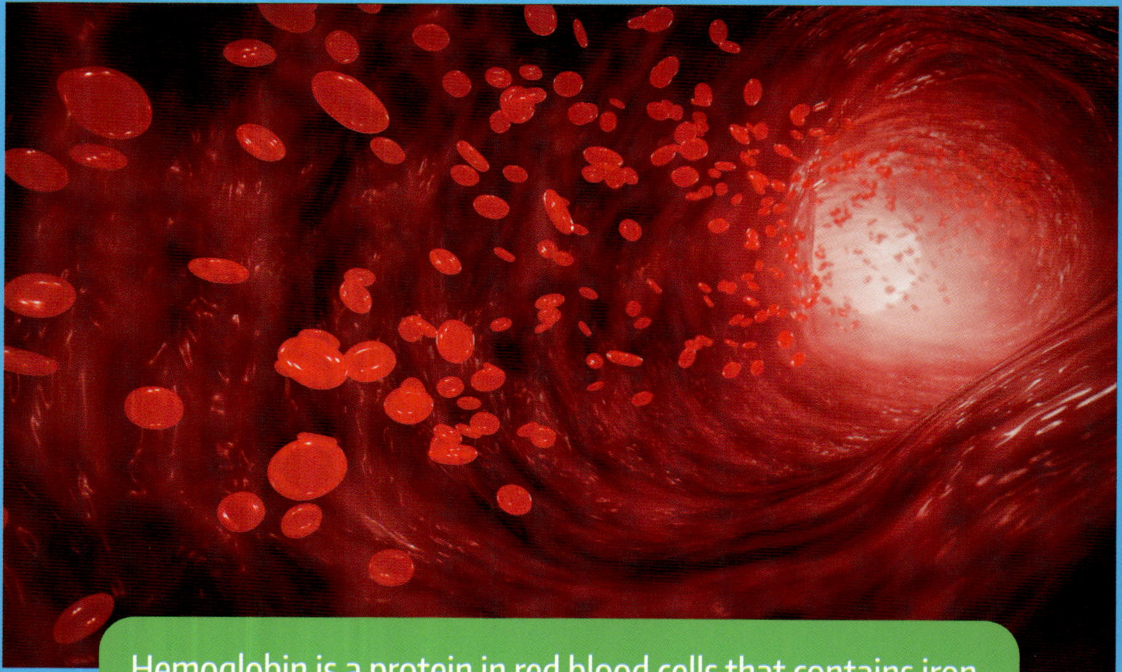

Hemoglobin is a protein in red blood cells that contains iron. Hemoglobin carries oxygen through the blood stream.

Eating a variety of foods guarantees that people get the nine essential amino acids.

Plants produce all twenty types of amino acid that they need. The human body, on the other hand, can make only eleven of the twenty required types. People need to get the other nine amino acids from the food they eat. These nine are known as the essential amino acids. They are histidine, isoleucine, leucine, lysine, methionine, phenylalanine, threonine, tryptophan, and valine.

WORD WISE

A SEQUENCE IS A SET ORDER IN WHICH THE SMALLER PARTS OF A BIGGER THING ARE ARRANGED.

What Are Fibrous Proteins?

There are two main kinds of proteins. Fibrous proteins are shaped like fibers, or threads. They are made up of long chains of amino acids that are arranged into strands or sheets.

Fibrous proteins are found in the fur, quills, scales, nails, feathers, horns, antlers, and hooves of animals. They also are a part of skin, including human skin. Fibrous proteins are found in bone, tendons, and cartilage as well. Tendons connect **muscles** to bones. Cartilage is the rubbery tissue that covers and protects bones at the joints.

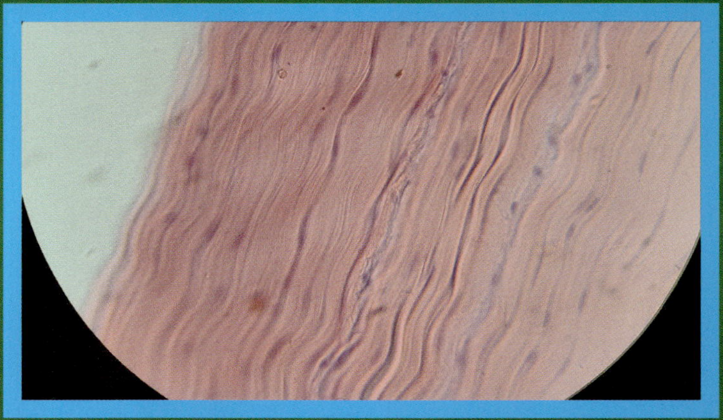

This is a microscopic view of the fibrous proteins in a human tendon.

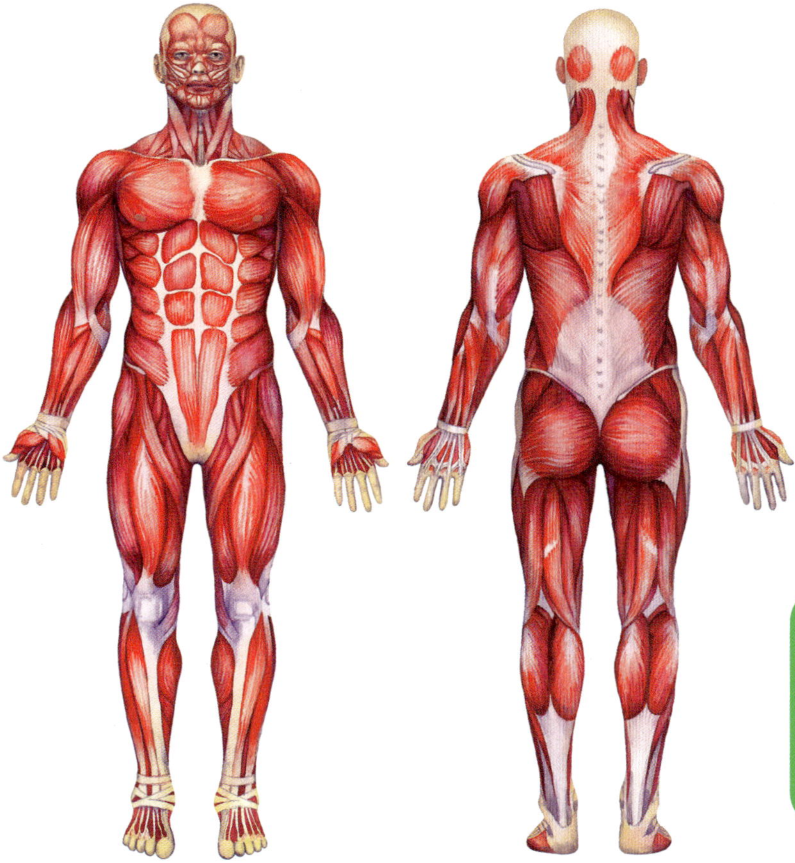

Actin and myosin are fibrous proteins that play a big role in helping muscles to move.

Collagen and elastin are fibrous proteins found in the deeper skin layers. Fibrin is a fibrous protein that binds blood platelets together to form blood clots. Clots plug holes that may develop in the walls of blood vessels. This action helps to stop bleeding.

WORD WISE

MUSCLES ARE THE BODY TISSUES THAT ANIMALS USE FOR MOVEMENT.

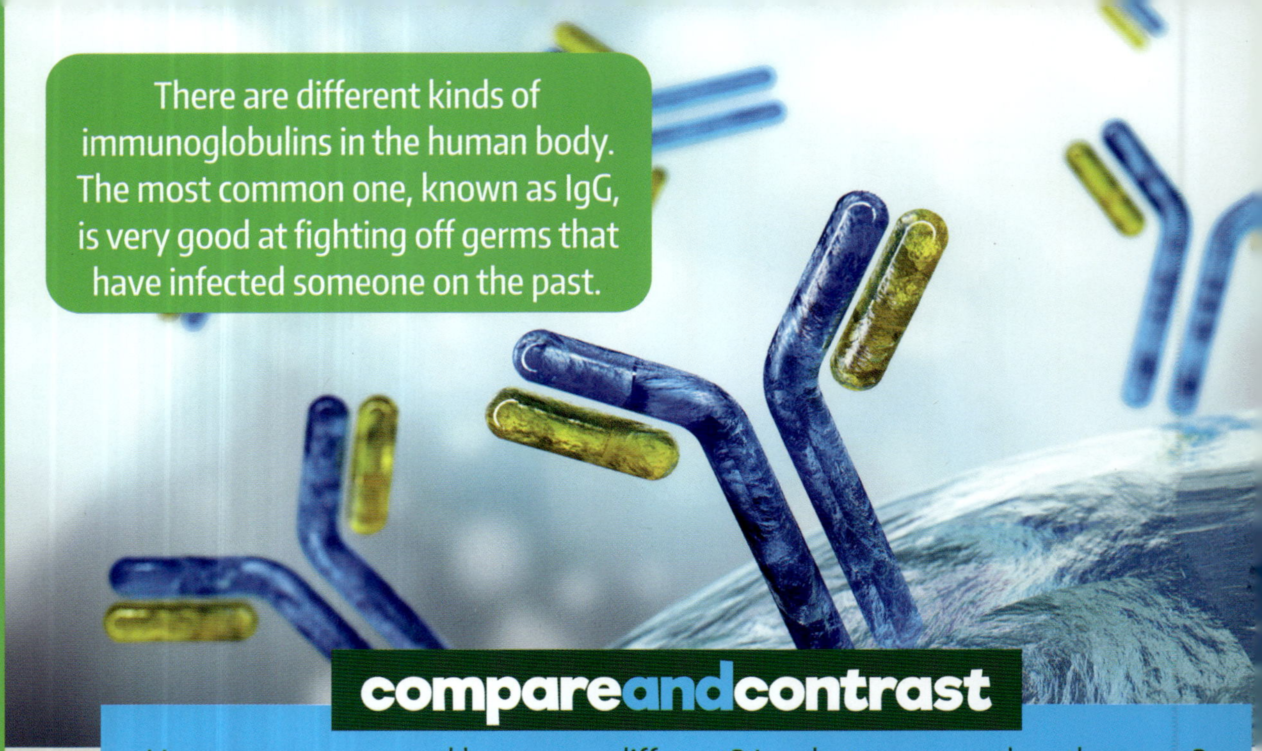

There are different kinds of immunoglobulins in the human body. The most common one, known as IgG, is very good at fighting off germs that have infected someone on the past.

compareandcontrast

How are enzymes and hormones different? In what ways are they the same?

People with a condition known as diabetes need to take man-made insulin regularly because their bodies don't make enough of it to regulate the levels of glucose in the blood.

What Are Globular Proteins?

The second kind of proteins are called globular proteins because they have a globe-like shape. The amino acid chains in globular proteins are folded up into a round structure. There are many kinds of globular proteins in the human body. Immunoglobulins, or antibodies, are one sort of globular protein. They fight harmful materials, such as germs, that enter the body.

Most enzymes are globular proteins. Enzymes are catalysts, or substances that control how quickly chemical reactions occur. Enzymes help the body to perform such tasks as digestion and growing new cells.

Some hormones are globular proteins. Hormones tell cells and body parts to do certain things. For example, hormones tell the body when to grow and when to stop growing. The hormones insulin and glucagon maintain safe levels of glucose in the blood. Glucose is a form of sugar used by the body.

Globular proteins known as transport proteins carry substances from one place in the body to another. Hemoglobin is a transport protein in red blood cells. It picks up oxygen as it moves through lung tissue and then carries it to the rest of the body. Other transport proteins are found in **cell membranes**. These proteins shuttle nutrients and waste products from one side of the membrane to the other.

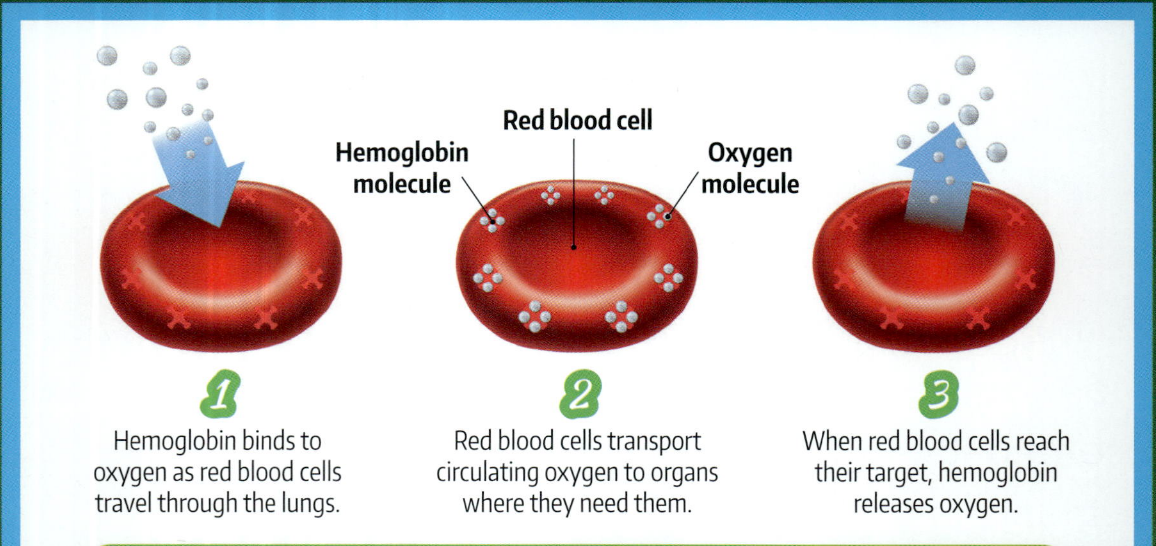

The hemoglobin in red blood cells picks up oxygen from the lungs and distributes it to the entire body via the bloodstream.

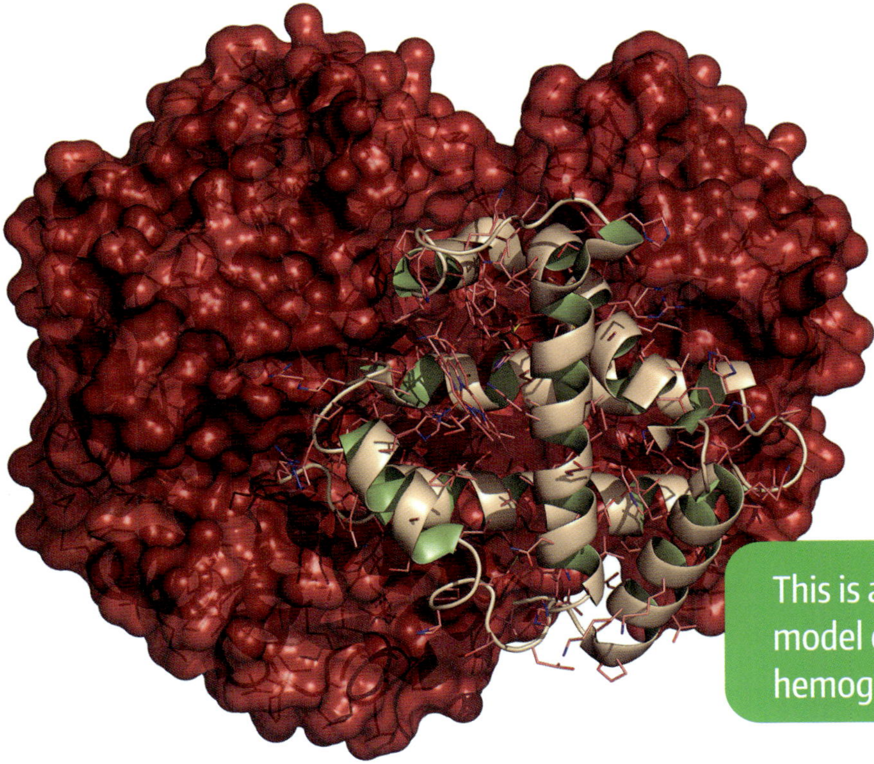

This is a three-dimensional model of a red blood cell with hemoglobin attached to it.

Many globular proteins have a regulatory function. They help to regulate, or control, processes in the body. Some regulatory proteins prevent the harmful buildup of the products of respiration, which is the process that cells use to get energy from nutrients. Others keep the levels of nutrients in tissues from falling too low.

WORD WISE

CELL MEMBRANES ARE THE THIN BUT TOUGH WALLS AROUND CELLS. THEY LET USEFUL SUBSTANCES ENTER CELLS. THEY BLOCK THE ENTRY OF HARMFUL SUBSTANCES.

Protein Sources

People get all the essential amino acids they need from animal sources. These foods include meat, poultry, fish, eggs, and dairy products, such as milk, yogurt, and cheese. They are complete proteins.

Some animal sources of protein are less healthy than others. For example, eating lots of processed meats is tied to higher rates of cancer. Bacon, cured ham, corned beef, canned meats, precooked meats, and sausages are processed meats. Processed meats also are linked to diabetes and heart disease.

Foods from plant sources are incomplete proteins. Plant proteins may lack some of the essential amino acids or have low levels of them. However, people can get all the essential amino acids by eating a mix of different protein-containing plant foods. Good plant sources of protein are nuts, seeds, legumes, and tofu. Legumes include peas, beans, and soybeans.

All these foods are healthy sources of protein.

compare and contrast

How are proteins from plants like those from animals? How are they different?

Tofu is a protein-rich food made from soybeans.

Vegetarians do not eat meat, so all or most of the protein in their diets comes from plants. Many nonvegetarians around the world also get protein from plant foods, which are often less expensive and lower in fat than meat.

Plant sources of protein include nuts, legumes, soy milk, and tofu. Broccoli has some protein, too.

Whey is the liquid that remains after the cheese-making process.

Some people add extra protein to their regular diet. One popular way to get extra protein is to use protein powder. Protein powder usually contains whey, soy, or **casein protein**. Whey and casein are present in milk, while soy comes from the soybean plant. People often make shakes with protein powder, or they mix it into other foods. Bodybuilders and other athletes use it to build up muscle. Protein powder can be a good source of protein for vegetarians, too.

WORD WISE

CASEIN PROTEINS ARE A GROUP OF CLOSELY-RELATED PROTEINS IN THE MILK OF MOST MAMMALS.

How Much Do We Need?

The amount of protein a person needs from their diet depends on many factors, including how old a person is and whether that person is male or female. In 2015, the U.S. Department of Agriculture (USDA) recommended that kids from ages nine to thirteen eat 34 grams (1.2 ounces) of protein each day. It recommended 46 grams (1.6 oz) per day for girls who are ages fourteen to eighteen and 52 grams (1.8 oz) for boys of the same age.

In 2026, the USDA updated their nutrition guidelines. The new guidelines stress the importance of eating proteins at every meal.

The U.S. Food and Drug Administration (FDA) requires all food products, like this can of tuna, to show nutritional facts on the label so everyone can make wise dietary choices.

A chicken breast has about 30 grams (1 oz) of protein, while a can of tuna has 40 grams (1.4 oz). A large egg has 6 grams (0.2 oz.) of protein, and a cup of milk has 8 grams (0.3 oz). A serving of tofu has 20 grams (0.7 oz) of protein.

Consider This

Why do you think teens need more protein than younger kids?

A Lack of Protein

Protein plays many essential roles in the body. It is particularly important for people who are active. In fact, doctors recommend that people eat a protein-rich food, such as yogurt or nuts, after exercise.

Body builders and other athletes use whey powder to make sure they are getting enough protein to grow and repair muscles after a workout.

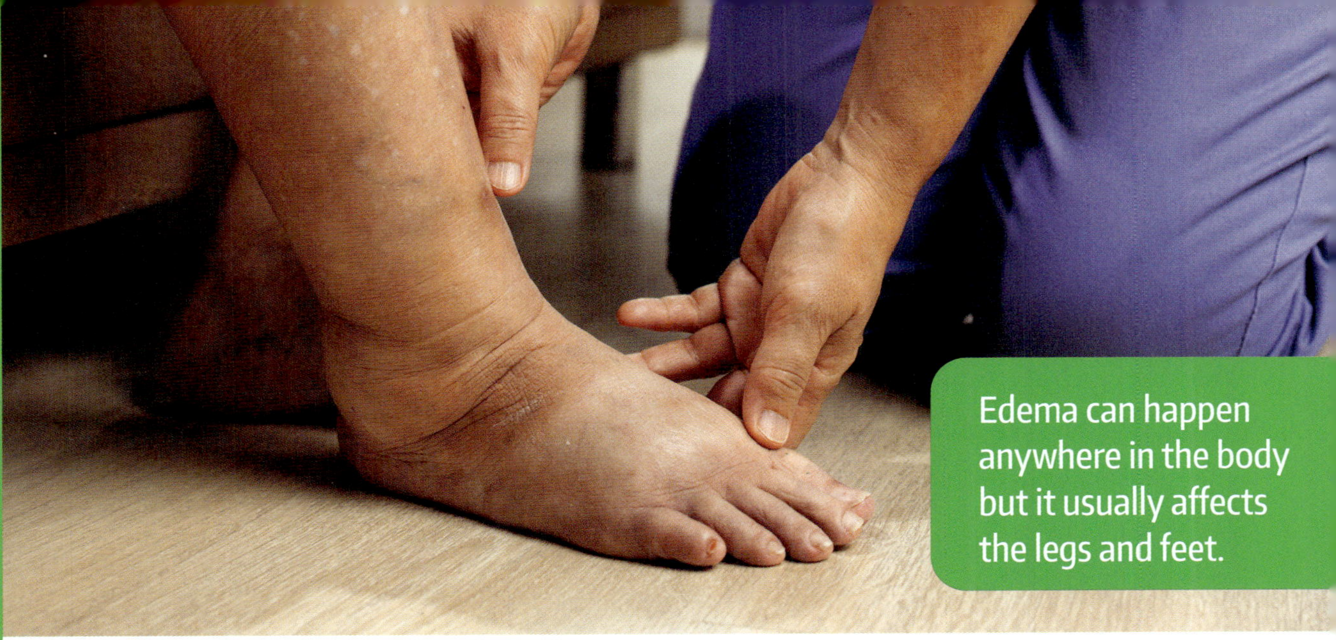

Edema can happen anywhere in the body but it usually affects the legs and feet.

If people do not eat enough protein, or if the proteins that they eat do not provide all the essential amino acids, problems can result. People who do not get enough protein may feel weak and tired. They also may lack muscle tone. Another clue that a person may not be getting enough protein is edema. Edema is a buildup of fluids that occurs most often in the legs and feet. Finally, a lack of protein can cause anemia, or problems with the body's red blood cells that can make a person feel weak and dizzy.

Consider This

Do you think you get enough protein? If not, how can you get more protein in your daily diet?

What Is Malnutrition?

Malnutrition is what happens to the body when a person does not get the right amount of nutrients. The most common form of malnutrition is protein-energy malnutrition. This type of malnutrition occurs when a person gets too little protein, too few **calories**, or both.

Kwashiorkor is a severe form of protein malnutrition. It is common among young children in developing countries. Children who suffer from kwashiorkor may get enough calories. They eat mostly starchy foods, such as cereal grains and cassava. However, these foods alone do not provide enough protein. Kwashiorkor causes weakness, anemia, failure to grow, and swelling of the belly.

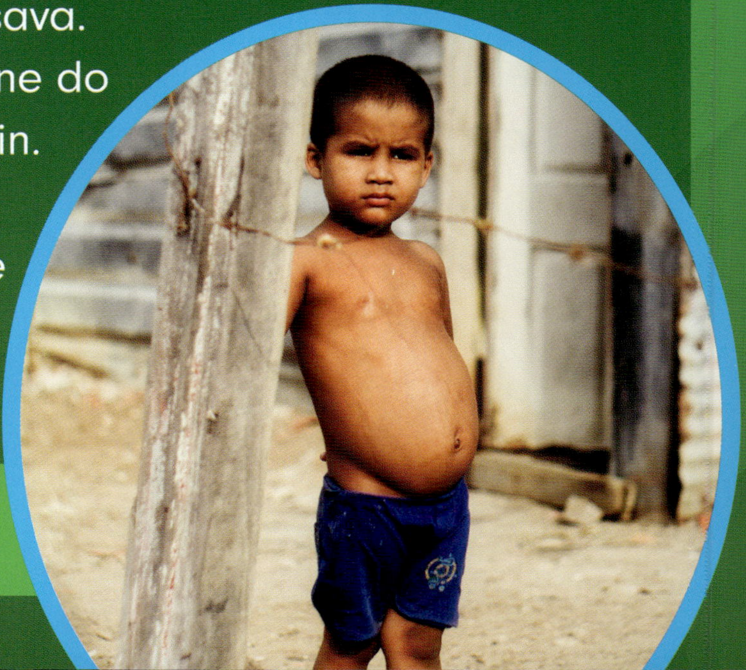

This boy shows the signs of kwashiorkor.

Marasmus occurs mostly among very young children, usually during famines when mothers produce less milk to feed their babies.

Marasmus is another kind of malnutrition. It results from not taking in enough protein and calories. Children with marasmus do not grow properly, and their fat and muscles waste away. Other symptoms include dehydration and dry, loose skin.

WORD WISE

THE AMOUNT OF ENERGY A FOOD CAN PRODUCE IS MEASURED IN CALORIES.

Too Much Protein

Diets that are very high in protein can damage the kidneys. People who eat too much protein also tend not to get enough of the other nutrients they need. For example, some protein-heavy diets do not provide the carbohydrates that the body requires. This lack of carbohydrates is unhealthy, especially in the long run.

Red meat is high in protein but it's also high in saturated fat. Eating too much red meat can result in heart problems and other health issues.

Fish is high in protein, and it also contains omega-3 fatty acids, which have been proven to improve cardiovascular health.

Diets with lots of protein from meat can be a problem, too. They tend to have more fat than is healthy. The USDA advises people who eat meat to choose low-fat or lean meats and poultry. It also recommends eating more fish, beans, peas, nuts, and seeds.

People who try to add extra protein to their diets do not always make healthy choices, either. For example, they may eat protein bars that are high in sugar.

Consider This

Most Americans consume more protein than their bodies need. Why do you think this happens?

The Primary Nutrient

Proteins are of primary importance to living things, and the body needs them to stay healthy. For that reason, it is necessary for people to include enough protein in their diets. The proteins in foods provide the amino acids that the body uses to make all the proteins it requires.

Some scientists study the proteins that the body makes. The exact number of protein types in the body is not known. So far, scientists have discovered many thousands.

The word "protein" comes from the Greek word proteios, which means "primary" or "first."

Proteins make spider silk stretchy and very strong.

Although proteins are essential to human health, they are useful to people for other reasons. Many commercial products contain proteins. For example, laundry detergents often contain the proteins called enzymes. The enzymes help to clean clothing by breaking down the proteins in stains. Proteins also may be found in some plastics.

Some useful proteins are made by scientists in labs! However, many useful proteins are found in nature. Manufacturers can get proteins from milk, spider webs, mushrooms, and other natural sources.

Consider This

If you were a scientist, what would you want to learn about proteins?

Glossary

abundant Existing in large numbers.
amino acid One of the building blocks from which proteins are made.
blood vessels A system of tubes that carry blood throughout the body.
cancer A disease that causes certain cells in the body to grow out of control.
carbohydrates Nutrients, such as starches and sugars, that give the body the energy it needs.
cardiovascular Of, relating to, or involving the heart and blood vessels.
cell The smallest unit with the basic properties of life.
chemical reaction The changing of matter into new types of matter.
dehydration The loss of water or other body fluids.
diabetes A disease caused by too much of a sugar called glucose in the body.
digestion The breaking down of food into a form that the body can use.
essential Totally necessary.
famine An extreme shortage of food in an area.
joint A place, such as the elbow, where the body can bend.
kidneys Body parts that create urine from waste that they remove from the blood.
lab A place where scientists work and do experiments.
legume One of several plants in the pea family, such as beans, peas, peanuts, and soybeans.
nutrient One of the things in food that the body needs to function and maintain itself.
platelet A small, round, thin blood cell that helps blood to stop flowing from a cut by forming thick and sticky clots.
tissue A group of cells that work together to do a specific job.

For More Information

Books

Kuehl, Ashley. *Nutrition*. Bloomington MN: SilverTip Books, 2025.

Rossiter, Brienna. *Proteins*. St. Paul, MN: North Star Editions, 2024.

Websites

How to Make Healthy Food Choices
kidshealth.org/en/kids/pyramid.html
Read all about nutrition and find links to similarly related topics.

How to Understand and Use the Nutrition Facts Label
www.fda.gov/food/nutrition-facts-label/how-understand-and-use-nutrition-facts-label
Read more about food labels and how to use them at this detailed website from the FDA.

Index